The Goldendoodle

STACY BRUSSEAU

This guide will help you further understand the goldendoodle breed; it is filled with goldendoodle facts and information, as well as training tips, detailed instructions, and healthcare advice.

AuthorHouse™
1663 Liberty Drive
Bloomington, IN 47403
www.authorhouse.com
Phone: 1-800-839-8640

© 2009 Stacy Brusseau. All rights reserved.

No part of this book may be reproduced, stored in a retrieval system, or transmitted by any means without the written permission of the author.

First published by AuthorHouse 5/26/2009

ISBN: 978-1-4389-7218-3 (sc)

Printed in the United States of America
Bloomington, Indiana

This book is printed on acid-free paper.

INTRODUCTION

Goldendoodles have been bred since the 1990s; they have become a very popular breed in many areas of the world, especially the United States. Goldendoodles are not yet recognized by the larger breed clubs, such as the American Kennel Club, but in time, they will be. I note that they are a breed simply because they have been intentionally bred; they are sold with pedigree so the lineage is known, and therefore, they are indeed a breed. These cute, happy, furry friends are going to be companions to humans for decades to come.

Introduction	1
Chapter 1 Is a Goldendoodle the Right Dog for You?	5
Chapter 2 Choosing a Breeder, the Right Breeder	8
Chapter 3 Goldendoodle Generations and Sizes	11
Chapter 4 Poodle and Golden Retriever Standards	13
Chapter 5 Hybrid Vigor	14
Chapter 6 Illness and Genetic Disorders	16
Chapter 7 Puppy Raising	18
Chapter 8 Health and Vaccinations	21
Chapter 9 Training	25
Chapter 10 Resources	29

Goldendoodles have a kind nature and keen ability to detect when their owners are in need of assistance, which has given them the advantage to be excellent therapy dogs, as well as beloved pets. Goldendoodles are very in tune to their human families; they will often detect when their owners are feeling down and rush to comfort them. Goldendoodles are very kind and family-oriented dogs; they have superior intelligence and can bond with anyone. They excel with children; goldendoodles are the type of dog that can endure any form of conduct from a child and still be as gentle as a teddy bear. The goldendoodle displays traits from both the golden retriever and the poodle, which results in a dog that is mostly non-shedding, mostly hypoallergenic, gentle, and compassionate and also an exceedingly intelligent dog.

Goldendoodles come in three different sizes, miniature, medium, and standard; therefore, the goldendoodle can accommodate any family and any lifestyle. For folks who reside in apartment or loft settings, the miniature goldendoodle is the type of dog that is not so big that it would get underfoot, and it can also be trained to use a litter box or a pad. Many apartments have regulations that state that the occupant cannot have a pet larger than twenty-five to thirty pounds; the miniature goldendoodle is typically less than twenty-five pounds, so the miniature would be an acceptable dog for an apartment. Although the goldendoodle can be found in three different sizes, their personalities remain static through the sizes; a miniature does not act the same as a small breed dog: it resembles a golden retriever in a multitude of ways and yet still has those unique qualities that goldendoodles possess.

Goldendoodles are often a preferred choice for families that have moderate to severe allergies. It is recommended to be sure to check with your breeder to see if his or her previous litters have been placed in homes that had one or more family members who suffered from allergies to dogs. I also recommend visiting a family that owns a goldendoodle, preferably a family who has a goldendoodle from your breeder's previous litter; inquire with your breeder to see if he or she could set up such a meeting. The higher the generation of goldendoodle, the more hypoallergenic and non-shedding the goldendoodle will be. For example, compare an F1 and an F1b: the F1 is a first generation, a fifty-fifty cross, mostly hypoallergenic and non-shedding, but look at the

F1b; this is a cross between an F1 goldendoodle and a poodle, so these goldendoodles will have more poodle than golden retriever traits, such as their coat, amplifying the hypoallergenic and non-shedding traits. For families that suffer from severe allergies, the F1b goldendoodle may be a wise choice.

Golden retrievers have been popular dogs because of their loving personalities and soft, furry coats; however, some golden retrievers shed heaps, and they tend to be large-scale dogs. Golden retrievers are also notorious for hip dysplasia. Maybe you have had a golden retriever who has passed away from a genetic disease, and now you are hesitant to get a new pet because you are worried that the same thing will happen all over again; well, the goldendoodle is the perfect dog for you. Poodles have been known to be very intelligent dogs; they learn fast and tend to develop a deep bond with their owners, much like the golden retriever. Goldendoodles have been found to have less congenital defects than both the golden retriever and the poodle, increasing their longevity and decreasing the chances of hip dysplasia, allowing you to have a pet that lives a long and healthy life. Goldendoodle offspring will be more intelligent and healthier than both of their parents.

Have you determined that the goldendoodle is the right dog for you yet? Read on and I will convince you further.

Breeders are ubiquitous; they are found splashed all over the classified section of the newspaper and on every puppy or breed search on the Internet. It is a very difficult choice to make to decide on one out of the thousands that pop out of the woodwork when you take the time to look for a dog. Once you have determined that the goldendoodle is the preferred breed of dog for you and your family, it is best to begin your search by gathering a list of reputable breeders of goldendoodles that seem to have informative Web sites or good descriptive advertisements in the local newspaper. Be sure to research your breeder; it never hurts to call around and ask a multitude of breeders before settling on one.

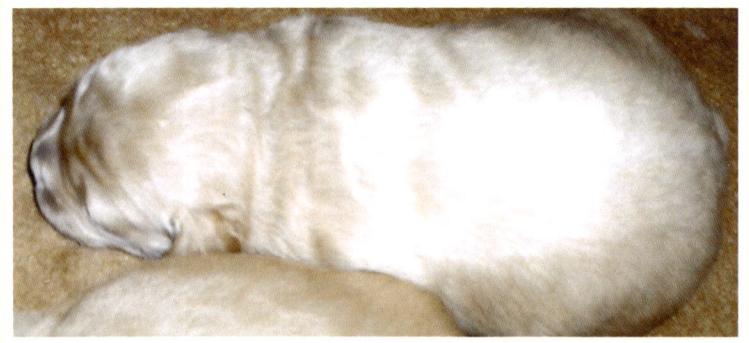

The qualities of a reputable breeder are vast: first and foremost, it is a benefit if your breeder is actually in the business of breeding dogs, not simply a once-a-year breeder. Choosing a breeder that is in the business of breeding a particular breed of dogs typically means that the breeder spends his or her life, day in and day out, working with his or her dogs. By breeding regularly, the breeder will have all his or her breeding stock up to date on vaccinations, he or she will have a regular veterinarian who will see the puppies, he or she will have a well-written contract for puppy purchase, and he or she will be more than willing to elucidate his or her vast knowledge of his or her dogs and the breed itself. I truly see a difference in professionalism as well as dog and puppy personalities when the breeder is dedicated to his or her dogs and puppies.

Do not be afraid of the prices of goldendoodles; some will be way out of line, but most will have a high but standard price. Remember that the cost of caring for these little babies is immense; many breeders will not give deals, and that is only fair to the other buyers to keep the pricing scheme stable. However, the price should reflect the breeder's reputability: if the breeder has health-tested breeding stock, a professional contract, and a two-year health guarantee, then most likely, the breeder is reputable, but there are other things to be aware of. First of all, a breeder should always be present and ready to assist when his or her bitch (female dog) whelps (delivers her puppies).

A breeder should be present for copulation to be sure that the dog and bitch do not injure themselves. A reputable breeder will also be very clean and keep his or her dogs and kennel neat and tidy. A breeder who prides him- or herself on his or her business will show it in his or her dogs.

Being a licensed and inspected breeder is a good quality to look for; typically local/state authorities issue licensing for pet dealers; this ensures that the breeder is frequently checked and that any activity he or she does regarding the sales/breeding of dogs is regulated. State authorities examine proper sanitation; this ensures the upkeep and health of the dogs, and also, in these cases, typically the law of the state will protect the buyer. Many states require licensing, so be sure to check with your local government to see if there is state licensing for pet dealers.

Make sure your breeder has a contract; typically, the contract duration is two years of the puppy's life. This means the breeder is truly concerned about his or her puppy and wants to be sure you will follow through on a few simple rules, such as getting the puppy fixed at five to six months, and letting the breeder know first if you were going to have to give up your puppy. Breeders should always care about where their puppies go, and who will take their puppies if the new owners are no longer able to care for the puppies. Contracts protect the puppy as well as the buyer and breeder.

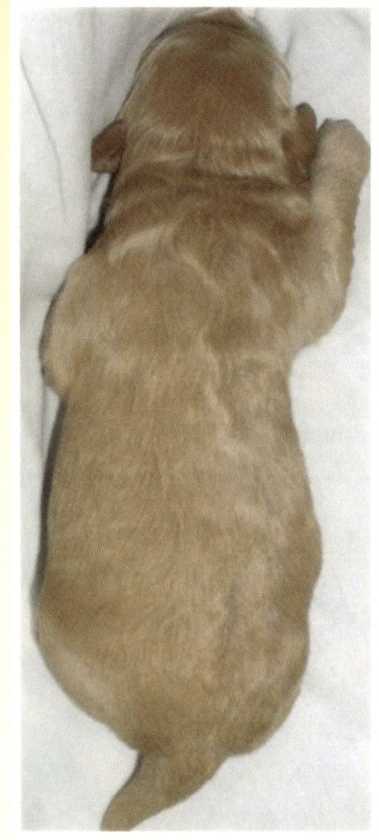

It is rare to find breeders who have Better Business Bureau (BBB) accreditation, but if you do find one with BBB accreditation, it will be a plus. Having BBB accreditation will protect the buyer; the BBB is there to mediate any legal situation that may arise and handle it out of court if at all possible.

It is essential that the breeder keep your puppy for eight weeks of his or her life; puppies need to learn from the littermates and mother. As for shipping, it is suggested not to ship a new puppy alone in an airplane; it is best if the puppy is delivered by car to his or her new home. Many breeders offer delivery for a minimal charge; it is worth the few extra dollars to take it. Last of all, when in doubt, ask for references; these should be from previous puppy owners and/or other breeders.

F-1 generations, or first generations, are a fifty-fifty cross between a poodle and a golden retriever; these dogs are mostly hypoallergenic and mostly non-shedding. The F1 has a playful disposition and typically mimics the golden retriever in many ways.

F1b generations are a cross between an F1 goldendoodle and a poodle. The F1b is a backcross; this will weed out the golden coat style and also some of the golden personality; however, it will keep the poodle coat style and allow the dog to be more hypoallergenic. F1b generation goldendoodles are sweet and gentle dogs; they still mimic a lot of the golden retriever traits but simply have a bit more

of a poodle coat style. F2 generation is a cross between an F1 goldendoodle and another F1 goldendoodle. F2b generation is a cross between an F1 goldendoodle and an F1b goldendoodle. F3 generations can be a cross between an F2b and another F2b, an F2 and an F2, or an F1b and another F1b.

As the goldendoodle generations increase, they tend to lose a great deal of their golden traits; however, they do become more and more hypoallergenic.

Every animal has some type of dander; it just so happens that people with asthma, emphysema, and allergies to most animals are often unaffected by the goldendoodle, even the F1 generation.

Goldendoodle sizes can vary; there are three main size ranges that they can be bred to be: miniature, medium, and standard. The height of any dog is measured at the withers, which is behind the neck around the area of the shoulder blades.

The miniature goldendoodle has a weight of approximately ten to twenty-five pounds and a height of approximately fourteen to twenty-one inches.

The medium goldendoodle has a weight of approximately thirty to forty-five pounds and a height of approximately sixteen to twenty-one inches.

The standard goldendoodle has a weight of approximately forty-five pounds and up and a height of approximately twenty-two to twenty-seven inches.

The personalities, although each dog is unique, can be quite similar between the size differences: miniature goldendoodles tend not to act like "purse dogs"; they will cuddle with you and can sit on your lap if that is what you are seeking, but they still possess the "big dog" traits. They will follow you around if you let them and they will play ball if you play with them and they will obey commands just like the golden retriever and poodle.

CHAPTER 4
Poodle and Golden Retriever Standards

The poodle comes in several sizes, which is why the goldendoodle can be bred to come in three distinct sizes.

Moyen poodles are typically twenty to thirty pounds and fifteen to twenty inches in height. Miniature poodles are typically fifteen to seventeen pounds and approximately ten to fifteen inches in height. Standard male poodles are forty-five to seventy pounds and fifteen inches and up. Standard female poodles are forty-five to sixty pounds and fifteen inches and up. Toy poodles are six to nine pounds and ten inches or less.

The golden retriever bitch (female dog) is typically between fifty-five to sixty-five pounds and twenty-one to twenty-two inches high. The golden retriever dog is typically sixty-five to seventy-five pounds and twenty-three to twenty-four inches high.

CHAPTER 5
Hybrid Vigor

The term "hybrid vigor" is also known as heterosis, or outbreeding enhancement. What this means is the offspring are seen as superior to their donors (parents). This is seen often in goldendoodle dogs, but a breeder is to be careful with this because both parents should still be tested for genetically predisposed disorders, and the disorders should be ruled out prior to breeding.

When crossing two inbred or closely bred animals of different breeds together, the offspring tend to be heterozygous, which simply means that the goldendoodle carries two separate copies of a gene, so it is not affected by many of the traits that homozygous[1] animals are affected by.

The hybrid dogs will often possess the dominant alleles[2] from one parent and suppress the recessive alleles from the other parent. This enables a hybrid to live a healthier life than its homozygous parent.

Second generations will have less hybrid vigor because they are the product of two of the same breed; often an F2 generation litter does not produce any uniformity, and often they can appear less attractive than the F1 generation.

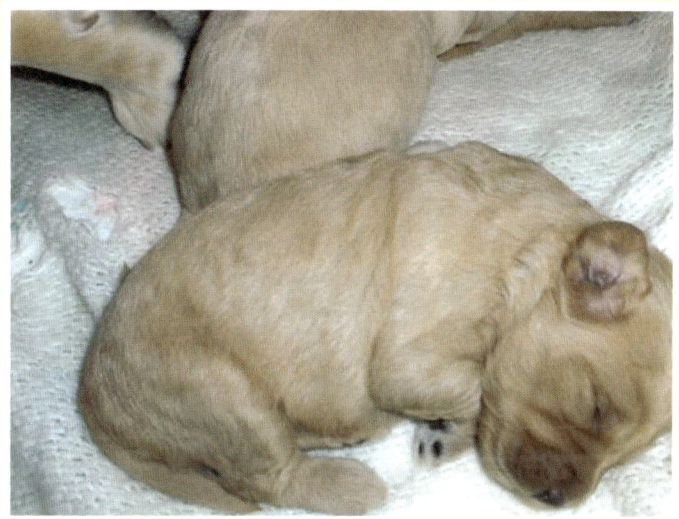

Notes
1. Homozygous means carrying identical forms of a gene.
2. Allele is a form of gene at a particular location on the animal's chromosomes.

CHAPTER 6
Illness and Genetic Disorders

Hip Dysplasia is a very common disorder in the golden retriever. Hip dysplasia is simply arthritis in the joints, but in a severe form, this debilitating disease can affect dogs in the most severe manner. It is essential that both the golden retriever and the poodle get tested through PennHIP[1] and/or OFA,[2] which are both specialty veterinary hip testing that will help the breeder rule out degenerative joint disease in his or her breeding stock.

Progressive retinal atrophy (PRA) is a very common eye disease that can be found in poodles; PRA affects the vascular system of the retina in the dog, and this leads to eventual blindness.

Cataracts are common in young golden retrievers; despite the fact that many dogs and humans

develop cataracts later in life, it can be genetically coded to appear in the young dog. The testing for cataracts is simple and is a fast test that can be conducted in a specialist's office; results will be determined in the office.

I also recommend breeders conduct a series of genetic testing. Genetic testing can determine if a dog has a trait that can be passed on to the offspring; if that is the case, that dog should not be bred.

1. PennHIP, or the University of Pennsylvania Hip Improvement Program, is a hip test that requires a radiograph of the degree of hip joint laxity.
2. OFA, or the Orthopedic Foundation for Animals, is a hip-testing facility that determines hip dysplasia in dogs.

Having a puppy in the house is an exhilarating yet arduous experience; it requires patience and consistency. While it seems that the puppy months will last ceaselessly, they are indeed gone in a fleeting moment. Time is of the essence for learning; therefore, teaching should begin the day you take your puppy home. Most breeders will have already begun teaching your puppy his or her name and that is an enormous help, but there is so much for puppy to learn.

To begin, your puppy must learn where to relieve his or her bladder and bowels, so begin by taking your puppy outside early in the morning, after meals, after play, after drinking water, and as close to bedtime as you can. When you take your puppy outside, it is best to take a treat with you and treat your puppy immediately after he or she goes potty outside; choose a treat that won't be too distracting; you want to be sure your puppy is going to actually go potty outside, not just wait for the treat; say the word "potty" as your puppy is going potty. If you were to treat

your puppy when he or she came indoors, then he or she will not understand what the treat is for. Don't rub your puppy's face in fecal or urinary matter after he or she goes potty indoors; just try to catch the dog right away and take him or her outside. Rubbing the puppy's face in the poop does nothing in terms of training, and if you do that, the puppy will most likely find a hidden place indoors to relieve him- or herself.

Discourage barking, jumping, and mouthing. Between four and six months of age, your dog will begin to lose teeth; this is normal. Your dog may swallow them, or you may find them on toys or on the carpet; this is very normal and so is the excessive chewing that you will find. This is a good time to invest in Nylabones and Kong toys to give your dog something to chew on besides your hands and clothes. Please do not think that your dog is attacking you; if there seems to be any abnormal behaviors, check with your veterinarian. Every time your dog goes to chew on you, simply replace the hand or non-dog object with a Nylabone or other related chew toy; this will help your dog understand the right thing to chew on. This stage will pass, but be sure to keep your dog on track and discourage the chewing on human skin or other non-dog items at all times.

Crate train or confine your puppy when you are not home or are sleeping. This will help your puppy learn where to go to the bathroom and where not to, as dogs typically do not wet where they sleep. So, crate at night and when you are not home; this will also help your puppy understand that he or she cannot chew on household items. Keep your puppy's crate in a central high-traffic location in your house so that your puppy can be with the family but also learn to sleep where there is much activity. Supervise your puppy at all times when he or she is out of the crate; puppies often go potty on carpet because it feels similar to grass; discourage this at all times. If your puppy whines in the crate in the middle of the night, only allow him or her out if you know he or she have to relieve him- or herself; if you start letting your puppy tell you when he or she wants out, then this whining will persist and carry over to everything your puppy wants! Use vinegar, bitter apple spray, lemon juice, or hot sauce to deter your puppy from chewing on various things and give your puppy lots of chew toys, Kong products, Nylabones, chew hooves, pig ears. The only downfall of chew hooves and pig ears is that they tend to have a pungent, objectionable odor. Try to avoid stuffed toys, especially those with hard eyes and noses or vinyl that can be easily swallowed.

  For feeding, keep the feeding location the same, as well as the sleeping place. Feed your puppy three times a day until six months or so, then check with your veterinarian to see when to switch from puppy food to adult food.

CHAPTER 8
Health and Vaccinations

G oldendoodles tend to be healthier than their parents, having hybrid vigor, but it is still essential to vaccinate for the general canine viruses. In this chapter, you will find it easy to navigate through; you will find the common canine viruses listed with their causes, signs, and treatment and a recommended vaccination schedule. If your veterinarian has you on a different schedule, please follow that schedule.

Canine distemper is often confused with the dog's temperament; this is extremely false. I often speak to people that seem to believe that the dog's personality will change when given the vaccination for distemper.

The distemper virus affects the respiratory, gastrointestinal, and neurological systems of the dog. The virus is transmitted via airborne pathway from respiratory secretions of infected animals. Distemper virus can affect wild animals, so it can be transmitted both from wild animals as well as domestic dogs. The most common dogs at risk are those who are under the age of four months and those who have not previously been vaccinated.

The signs of distemper virus are frequent ocular (eye) discharge, from watery to puss-like secretions; fever; nasal discharge; cough; lethargy; decrease in appetite; emesis (vomiting); and diarrhea. In the later stages of the virus, the dog may experience seizures, twitching, and then paralysis.

Those who contract distemper virus will be treated for the secondary infections; there is no treatment for the virus itself. Distemper is often fatal. The best way to prevent a dog from contracting distemper is to vaccinate in four-week intervals starting around six to eight weeks of age and ending around fourteen to sixteen weeks of age.

Canine parvo virus is a highly contagious virus that affects the gastrointestinal system of puppies and unvaccinated adult dogs. Wild animals can also carry this virus, and it can be transmitted between domestic dogs and wild animals. Parvo can be contracted by exposure to contaminated feces; it can also be spread from surfaces such as food bowls and flooring. Parvo is resistant to hot and cold temperatures, as well as humid and dry environments. Parvo can also last an exceptionally long amount of time under those circumstances, lasting for months to years. The greatest risk lies with puppies four months and younger and unvaccinated dogs. The major signs of parvo virus are lethargy, decreased appetite, fever, emesis, and bloody diarrhea. The vomiting and diarrhea can cause sudden dehydration. By the time the signs are noticed, it is typically followed by death within twenty-four to forty-eight hours. After a diagnosis through a fecal test, the dog can be treated with a treatment plan, including increasing electrolytes and immune system support. There is no drug that can kill the virus, so even with a positive early diagnosis, the results are typically grim; death is ultimately the conclusion. If a dog, however, does

survive the virus, he or she will shed the virus for weeks to months from his or her stool, so isolation is essential. The best way to prevent this debilitating disease is to vaccinate in three- to four-week intervals starting around six to eight weeks of age and ending around fourteen to sixteen weeks of age.

Hepatitis is a contagious disease in dogs that can be spread via feces, urine, and saliva. This disease affects the liver, kidneys, spleen, and lungs. The dogs that are most at risk are those who are under four months and those who have not previously been vaccinated. The signs of hepatitis are fever, fast heartbeat, anorexia, extreme thirst, and eye and nose discharge. Hepatitis can be detected by a change in the liver and gallbladder; treatment can include blood transfusion and IV fluids. The best way to prevent this devastating disease is to vaccinate in four-week intervals starting around six to eight weeks of age and ending around fourteen to sixteen weeks of age.

Leptospirosis is more common in certain areas, so it is best to inquire with your veterinarian regarding the necessity for this vaccination. It can be transmitted from wild animals, so it is best to keep the dog vaccinated when in a rural area. The signs are fever, depression, lethargy, anorexia, ocular and nasal discharge, emesis, diarrhea, and inflammation of the nervous system. A diagnosis can be made through serology, and treatment would be to treat the renal and liver failure with an increase of fluids and antibiotics. The best prevention is once again to vaccinate all puppies and, every three years after the first year vaccination, to revaccinate your dog.

Parainfluenza is an airborne virus that can cause a cough, nasal discharge, increased respirations, increased rate of breath, resulting in bacterial pneumonia. The treatment is antimicrobial therapy to kill the bacteria. The best way to prevent this is also to vaccinate.

Vaccinations should be given starting between six weeks and eight weeks of age; typically, the distemper, hepatitis, parvo, and parainfluenza vaccines are given starting at six weeks; the leptospirosis is typically skipped in the first series of vaccination, but it will begin on the second, which is around ten weeks of age, and is then completed on the third vaccination between fourteen and sixteen weeks of age. Dogs should be vaccinated with a modified live virus to give the best immunity; they should be vaccinated one year following the last of the series of three and then every three years following unless it is recommended sooner by a veterinarian. Rabies vaccinations are typically given at three months of age; your veterinarian will advise you if your state of residence requires it sooner or later than three months.

T raining any dog is an essential part of being a responsible dog owner; to start, it is best to use positive reinforcement to train your dog; what this means is using praise and rewards to reinforce the dog's good behaviors. Using positive reinforcement training can be accomplished in a safe and rewarding fashion, rather than using force, which can hurt the bond between dog and owner. Positive reinforcement will enable the owner to create a bond with his or her dog, rather than having his or her dog fear him or her. The old style of training was to use corrections and pinch, prong, or choke chains to train; however, that has been found to be unsuccessful with many

household breeds, as well as being less humane. Dogs have become parts of our families rather than watchdogs or working dogs.

To teach *sit*, it is best to choose a quiet room in the house, gather up some treats and your dog. Crouch or sit on the floor while practicing; this will enable you to be closer to your dog and control the encouragement to jump up for the treat. Hold the treat in your hand, close to your dog, and starting out with your dog in a standing position, gradually raise the treat (your hand) above your dog, letting your dog's nose follow the treat. When your dog's butt touches the ground, give the treat and say the word "sit," then praise your dog. Timing is everything, so try to do this in a timely fashion.

To teach *down*, there are two ways to do it: the first is to start with your dog in a sitting position, hold the treat at your dog's nose, and gradually let your dog's nose follow the treat to the ground; bringing the treat towards the ground in a straight line is best; this is easiest if practiced on a linoleum or tile floor rather than a carpet. When your dog's front elbows touch the ground, say the word "down," then treat and praise your dog. The second way to teach *down* is best for a smaller dog, such as a mini goldendoodle. Sit on the floor with your legs straight out in front of you, but allow room between your legs; lure your dog to one side of your body with the treat; hold the treat under the knee of your leg; let your dog follow the treat as you guide your dog under your leg; your dog should follow. When your dog goes under your leg, he or she will be crouching or lying down; if your dog is crouching, just push down with a little pressure from your leg to guide your dog into a down position. As soon as your dog is down, elbows and butt planted on the ground, say the word "down" and treat and praise your dog.

When you are training commands such as *down* and *sit*, it is always best to use a fast word with as few syllables as possible so that your dog can understand the word. Also, remember not to use the word "down" for jumping; use the term "off" instead; this will prevent confusion. Try to stay consistent among family members and make sure every family member is using the same words. Practice these commands at least three times a day every day; try to practice in different locations so that your dog will learn to listen to the commands in every area of the house, as well as outside. Remember, consistency and repetition are the key to your dog's learning.

For jumping, it is best to turn away when your dog jumps and try to ignore it, regardless of how cute your dog looks at you. If jumping becomes a persistent problem, you can create a shaker can with pennies and shake it when your dog jumps; be sure to only use this can after your dog has graduated from his or her sensitive period; he or she should be older than three months when you begin using the can. To create the can, take an old soda can, rinse it out, and let it dry. Take about seven pennies and slip them in the can; cover the top of the can with tape so that the pennies do not fall out. Now, when your dog jumps, simply shake the can once and turn away. In time, your dog should cease jumping. Also, remember to get down to your dog's level to greet him or her; this will help your dog be able to see you and reduce the jumping.

For the *stay* command, the prerequisite is for the dog to know the *sit* and/or the *down* command, depending on which one you are planning on practicing. So to start to teach a *sit stay*, begin with your dog in a sitting position; say the word "stay," and ever so gradually, inch yourself away; don't go far away, and make sure you don't ask your dog to stay too long; he or she will not when he or she is learning; this is a complex process that takes time. Hold your hand up like a stop sign in front of your dog's nose and say the word "stay"; inch back a couple of inches, hold your treat out, and call your dog to come. This will help you work two commands at once, the *stay* and the *come*; you are also getting practice with the *sit* or *down* as well.

Brusseau, Stacy. "Golden Beauties. . . Driven to Doodles." Brusseau, Stacy. http://www.goodlepups.com

Thaboune, Trina. "Trina's Doodles and Poodles Quality Puppies from our Heart to Yours." Thaboune, Trina. http://www.tiggerdoodle.com

Stacy Brusseau has been a canine behavior consultant for close to a decade, specializing in aggression management. She began breeding goldendoodles after recognizing their kind temperament and intriguing qualities. Stacy owns Golden Beauties … Driven to Doodles breeding, which is located in upstate New York; she is a licensed and inspected breeder with the NYS Department of Agriculture and Markets (#638).

LaVergne, TN USA
03 January 2009
168780LV00002B